I don't know what I'm doing

Dominique Careddu

 BookLeaf Publishing

Presentation by *BookLeaf Publishing*

Web: www.bookleafpub.com

E-mail: info@bookleafpub.com

ISBN: 9789357212533

First edition 2023

My two kiddos. I hope I didn't mess you up too badly. Love you forever and ever.

ACKNOWLEDGEMENT

The universe that throws me through black holes and star births.

PREFACE

I have no idea. Enjoy:)

Lullaby of a single mom

Quiet night
Should feel calm
Should feel peace

Not right
The shame seeps
The guilt leaks

Hind sight
Be better tomorrow
Try and get some sleep

The story

My sister tells it best
Eyes wide with a laugh
Little bit of distaste
Little bit of impressed

It was a stormy winter day
Dangerous weather
A blizzard pretty much
And I wanted to play

Get your gear
Grab your board
Jump in the car
No four wheel drive
Eyes bright no fear

We're driving to a mountain
When no one else dared be out
As she tells it I just casually mention
Oh yeah by the way I'm pregnant

Then on the hill
She struggles and falls
Sliding down a "black diamond"
Unable to stop

I'm just laughing and playing
Carving circles around her

Daddy

My breath
It echoes in this room
It's all that I can do
And it just echos in this room

Her tears
They echo in this room
They're all that she can do
And they just echo in this room

Your spirit
It echoes in this room
You did all that you could do
You still echo in this room

Stuffed

5

All my good intentions
Are hiding in the cupboard

So many things I mean to do
But I don't have the time for

Serendipity

A story three years old

A chance excursion

Overheard it being told

I heard his screams

All that time ago

He met God

When he was a guy I didnt know

Three shooting stars

One of them green

Two months apart

But both the 22nd it seems

Charts say past lives

Rebirth

Falling pieces
All around
Knees hitting
Cold hard ground

Fingers scratching
Reaching claw
Eyes dripping
But filled with awe

Day end

Watching the sun sink
Blanket of orange putting the sky to sleep

Wish to you a goodnight
Till morning you carry my daydreams

I promise

Weather I like it or not
You have a spot

On my boat...

When the floods come
And the fires
The end of the world

You have a place with me

I could never leave you to swing
Never leave you to burn

Never leave you out to sea

Little peace

Rusty ships
And seagull calls
Rocks and sand
White gurgles

Rhythmic waves
Little pools from yesterday
Misty and foggy
Light came out to play

The armour

People think
I wear all my scars on my sleeve
My greatest trick
Make you think
That's all there is to see

Scars on my right
Heart on the left
Seem so open you don't ask
What's under the vest

Bullet proof
Love proof
Pounded steel
Guarding my wishes
My dandelion fields

Warrior woman

Pain and tears
Blood and sweat
Smiles and fears
Not quite there yet

People see the fight
They see the strength
While I just struggle
While I still sink

So much work
Such a steep climb
Guess cause I don't give up
They think I'm fine

I want princess or Goddess
Peace and ease in my life
But that's not my path
My way is to strive

Long game

The long game is the only one I know
Nothing ever came fast
You see the steps I make today
Think you know a better way
This is not fifteen minutes of fame
I play the long game

I'd trust your bagels

First you said donuts
How did you know?
Bagels and cream cheese next
How far will you go?

I'm a girl that takes coffee
As a gesture grand
All this extra
Makes me question your plans

You say I deserve it
And I certainly do
So yeah...
I'd take bagels from you

My universe

Dark waters
Dark matter
Drops of mercury
Drops of games

There is no cold
Only absence of heat
There is no Dark
Only absence of light

The muck

The tears froze on my face
Mind lost in time and space
Body stuck in place

Been down here so long
Adapted to survive
Learned how to breathe in the mud
Now I choke when I try
Starting to rise above

Flashlight

You were doing repairs
In the dark over there
And I held the light
I held the light

You felt
Broken
Lost
Scared
I held the light
I held the light

I'm in love with a mountain

Atop a snowy Ridge
Gazing a cross at a place
Where even the trees don't grow

Large valley below
Mountains all around lakes
And space
Where things are left to grow

Usually wrapped in the clouds
Your power and beauty forgotten
Can't take my eyes off you
Tall, strong, standing alone
A privilege not given often

First best friend

I'm happy for you
More than I'm sad about it
Put on a good show
But I promise you this
You are the one
I've always
Missed

Do you remember
Our wedding
When we were just kids
Now older
Still know eachother
But oh how much
Time we've
Missed

9 789357 212533